American black bear

NO LONGER PROPERTY OF SEATTLE PUBLIC LIBRARY

Spectac

PRIORITY
AIR MAIL

D0578090

BEAR BEAR
FEB 28

BY AIR MAIL
par avion

25

brown bear

NORTHGATE LIBRARY
AUG -- 2018

Asian
black bear

BBR

PAWPAW
11-05-16

1 They love to snack

Some bears love honey so much they rip open trees to reach a beehive—and even lap up the bees. But bears don't stick to honey. They eat all kinds of food.

sun bear

SHOW YOU LOVE A BEAR

Don't tempt a hungry bear! Human food is not good for them, so if you are camping in bear country, keep food out of the way.

hive

nest

hornbill

From berries and bark to fish and meat, bears eat whatever they can find. Only giant pandas are different— they just chew on bamboo.

② They build cozy dens

Bears make comfortable places to sleep. They dig out dens in hollows beneath tree roots or make nests in caves to escape the rain.

rain

den

forest floor

roots

Asian black bear

Some Asian black bears build day beds in trees while polar bears make dens in snowdrifts. Den-making bears like secret, quiet places where they can sleep in peace.

3 They can sleep for months

In winter, when it is difficult to find food, some bears go into a deep sleep to save energy. Hibernating in their dens, they can sleep for 100 days without eating and drinking. Their breathing slows down and their hearts hardly beat at all.

hillside

wildflowers

snow melt

den

cub

In spring, as the weather warms, bears wake up. Pregnant female bears give birth in their dens and only come out when there is enough food for their cubs to eat.

4 They give piggyback rides

A mother bear is loving and strict. She teaches her cubs all they need to know. Fiercely protective, she keeps them close. The cubs ride piggyback or are carried gently in their mother's mouth.

cubs

sloth bear

termites

Sri Lankan
jungle fowl

mango tree

Bear cubs are full of mischief and endlessly curious.
By watching their mother, these furry playmates
learn to find food and keep safe. They may all stay
together for as long as three years.

Steller's jay

black bear

SHOW YOU LOVE A BEAR

Do a wiggly dance! Browse online to see videos of bears scratching and scenting on their favorite trees.

porcupine

5 They wiggle and dance

Bears scratch their backs against trees to leave smells for other bears to find. By rubbing the bark, they post messages along their familiar forest trails. These marks may help them attract a mate or scare off a rival.

pine marten

cub

Most bears do a strange upright dance on their hind legs to leave their scent. But some giant panda bears aim higher and do a handstand to leave their mark!

They are terrific trackers

Bears have a much better sense of direction than humans. The polar bear is the greatest tracker of all. Like a mysterious compass in its shaggy head, instinct leads this wanderer home across the ice.

polar bear

seal pup

harp seal

With a sense of smell over 2,000 times better than ours, a bear can sniff food from 20 miles away. A polar bear can even smell the breath of a seal deep under the ice.

puffin

killer whale

7 They can surprise with a sprint

Bears look clumsy and slow. But an angry grizzly, a type of brown bear, sprints faster than a racehorse! Bears can run fast if they are hungry or mad. They can gallop uphill and downhill, but not for long. With their thick coats, bears quickly get hot and soon slow down.

cubs

grizzly bear

Only the giant panda, with very little energy from eating endless bamboo, doesn't run at all.

elk

lake

horsetail plant

8 They love a dip

Whether splashing around or just soaking, bears enjoy water. They paddle in lakes and rivers to escape biting insects, hunt for fish, or cool off on hot days. But one bear swims to survive...

iceberg

The polar bear can swim hundreds of miles to find ice thick enough to hold its weight. It hauls itself out onto the ice to hunt, catching seals as they come up for air.

SHOW YOU LOVE A BEAR

Help stop climate change! Global warming is melting Arctic ice, so polar bears are forced to swim farther and farther to find food.

Arctic char

polar bear

9 They hum in peace

From snorting and growling to grunting and coughing, bears make all kinds of noises that other bears understand. And if all is well, mother bears and their cubs just hum happily.

spectacled bear

bromeliad

Bears also use their bodies to show how they feel. They stand and stare, twist away, move their ears, sniff the air, charge forward, or lie down and relax.

owl butterfly

clouds

prickly pear

SHOW YOU LOVE A BEAR

Make some noise about bears! Tell your friends amazing bear facts so they learn to love them too.

They can be saved!

Living in remote forests in China, the giant panda is one of the rarest bears of all. This unusual bear bleats rather than growls and only ever eats bamboo.

giant panda